HEART-HEALTHY COOKBOOK

LOW-SODIUM, LOW-CHOLESTEROL RECIPES FOR A HEALTHY HEART

Emma Grace

TABLE OF CONTENT

1. GRILLED SALMON WITH LEMON AND GARLIC

Prep Time: 10 mins
Cook Time: 12 mins
Total Time: 22 mins
Servings: 4

Ingredients:

- 4 salmon fillets (6 oz every)
- 2 tbsp olive oil
- 2 tbsp lemon juice
- 2 cloves garlic, chop-up
- 1 tsp salt
- ½ tsp black pepper
- 1 tsp dried oregano
- ½ tsp red pepper flakes (non-compulsory)
- Lemon slices (for garnish)
- Fresh parsley (for garnish)

Instructions:

1. Set the grill's temperature to medium-high.
2. Combine the olive oil, lemon juice, garlic, oregano, salt, pepper, and red pepper flakes in a mini bowl.
3. After applying the marinade to the salmon fillets, leave them for five mins.
4. The salmon Must be cooked through after 5 to 6 mins of grilling it skin-side down and then flipping it over and cooking it for another 5 to 6 mins.
5. Take off the grill, sprinkle with parsley and lemon slices, and serve.

Nutrition (Per Serving):

Cals: 320, Protein: 34g

Carbs: 2g

Fat: 18g

2. BAKED COD WITH HERBS AND OLIVE OIL

Prep Time: 10 mins
Cook Time: 15 mins
Total Time: 25 mins
Servings: 4

Ingredients:

- 4 cod fillets (6 oz every)
- 3 tbsp olive oil
- 2 tbsp lemon juice
- 2 cloves garlic, chop-up
- 1 tsp dried thyme
- 1 tsp dried oregano
- ½ tsp salt
- ½ tsp black pepper
- ½ tsp paprika
- Lemon wedges (for serving)

Instructions:

1. Turn the oven on to 400°F, or 200°C.
2. Combine the olive oil, lemon juice, paprika, garlic, thyme, oregano, salt, and pepper in a bowl.
3. Cod fillets Must be put on a parchment paper-lined baking pan.
4. Apply the prepared Mixture to the fillets.
5. Fish Must flake easily with a fork after 12 to 15 mins in the oven.
6. Serve with slices of lemon.

Nutrition (Per Serving):

Cals: 220, Protein: 35g

Carbs: 1g

Fat: 9g

3.QUINOA-STUFFED BELL PEPPERS

Prep Time: 15 mins
Cook Time: 30 mins
Total Time: 45 mins
Servings: 4

Ingredients:

- 4 bell peppers, halved and seeds take outd
- 1 cup cooked quinoa
- 1 can (15 oz) black beans, drained and rinsed
- 1 cup diced tomatoes
- 1 tsp olive oil
- 1 mini onion, diced

- 1 clove garlic, chop-up
- 1 tsp cumin
- ½ tsp salt
- ½ tsp black pepper
- ½ cup shredded cheese (non-compulsory)
- Fresh cilantro (for garnish)

Instructions:

1. Turn the oven on to 375°F, or 190°C.
2. Heat the olive oil in a pan over medium heat. Sauté the garlic and onions up to they are tender.
3. Add the cumin, chop-up tomatoes, black beans, cooked quinoa, salt, and pepper.
4. Spoon the quinoa Mixture into every side of the bell pepper.
5. Cover the filled peppers with foil after placing them in a roasting dish.
6. Bake for twenty-five mins. Take off the foil, top with cheese if using, and continue baking for five more mins.
7. Serve after adding some fresh cilantro as a garnish.

Nutrition (Per Serving):

Cals: 260, Protein: 10g

Carbs: 42g

Fat: 6g

4.LENTIL AND SWEET POTATO STEW

Prep Time: 15 mins
Cook Time: 40 mins
Total Time: 55 mins
Servings: 4

Ingredients:

- 1 cup dry lentils, rinsed
- 1 Big sweet potato, peel off and diced
- 1 mini onion, diced
- 2 cloves garlic, chop-up
- 1 can (15 oz) diced tomatoes
- 4 cups of vegetable broth
- 1 tsp cumin
- 1 tsp paprika
- ½ tsp salt

- ½ tsp black pepper
- 1 tbsp olive oil
- Fresh parsley (for garnish)

Instructions:

1. Heat the olive oil in a saucepan over medium heat. Add the garlic and onion and cook up to tender.
2. Add the chop-up sweet potato, lentils, tomatoes, cumin, paprika, salt, pepper, and vegetable broth.
3. Bring to a boil, then lower the heat and simmer up to the lentils and sweet potatoes are cooked, stirring periodically, 35 to 40 mins.
4. Serve hot, garnished with fresh parsley.

Nutrition (Per Serving):

Cals: 290, Protein: 14g

Carbs: 50g

Fat: 5g

5.WHOLE WHEAT PASTA WITH ROASTED VEGETABLES

Prep Time: 10 mins
Cook Time: 30 mins
Total Time: 40 mins
Servings: 4

Ingredients:

- 8 oz whole wheat pasta
- 1 zucchini, split
- 1 red bell pepper, split
- 1 yellow bell pepper, split
- 1 mini eggplant, diced
- 2 tbsp olive oil
- 2 cloves garlic, chop-up
- ½ tsp salt
- ½ tsp black pepper
- 1 tsp dried Italian seasoning
- ½ cup cherry tomatoes, halved
- ¼ cup finely grated Parmesan cheese (non-compulsory)

Instructions:

1. Turn the oven on to 400°F, or 200°C.
2. Add olive oil, garlic, salt, black pepper, and Italian seasoning to the bell peppers, eggplant, and zucchini.
3. Arrange the veggies on a baking pan and roast them for twenty-five mins.
4. In the meantime, prepare pasta as directed on the box/pkg. After draining, set away.
5. In a bowl, combine the cooked pasta, cherry tomatoes, and roasted veggies. Throw well.
6. If using, top with Parmesan cheese and serve warm.

Nutrition (Per Serving):

Cals: 350, Protein: 12g

Carbs: 55g

Fat: 9g

6. LENTIL AND VEGETABLE SOUP

Prep Time: 15 mins
Cook Time: 40 mins
Total Time: 55 mins
Servings: 6

Ingredients:

- 1 cup green or brown lentils, rinsed
- 1 tbsp olive oil
- 1 onion, chop-up
- 2 carrots, diced
- 2 celery stalks, chop-up
- 3 cloves garlic, chop-up
- 1 can (14.5 oz) diced tomatoes
- 6 cups of vegetable broth
- 1 tsp cumin
- 1/2 tsp paprika
- 1/2 tsp dried thyme
- 1/2 tsp salt
- 1/4 tsp black pepper
- 2 cups of chop-up spinach or kale
- Juice of 1/2 lemon

Instructions:

1. In a Big saucepan, heat the olive oil over medium heat. Add the celery, carrots, and onion. For five mins, sauté.
2. Add the paprika, thyme, cumin, and garlic. For one min, stir.
3. Add the veggie broth, diced tomatoes, and lentils. After bringing to a boil, lower the heat and simmer for half an hr.
4. Add lemon juice and spinach/kale and stir. Cook for an additional five mins.
5. Serve hot after adjusting the seasoning.

Nutrition (Per Serving):

Cals: 190, Protein: 10g

Carbs: 30g

Fiber: 10g, Fat: 3g

7.TOMATO AND BASIL SOUP WITH OLIVE OIL

Prep Time: 10 mins
Cook Time: 30 mins
Total Time: 40 mins
Servings: 4

Ingredients:

- 2 tbsp olive oil
- 1 onion, chop-up
- 3 cloves garlic, chop-up
- 4 cups of ripe tomatoes, chop-up (or 1 can 28 oz crushed tomatoes)
- 2 cups of vegetable broth
- 1/2 tsp salt
- 1/4 tsp black pepper
- 1 tsp dried oregano
- 1/2 tsp red pepper flakes (non-compulsory)
- 1/4 cup fresh basil leaves, chop-up
- 1/2 cup heavy cream or coconut milk (non-compulsory)

Instructions:

1. In a saucepan, heat the olive oil over medium heat. Sauté the garlic and onion for five mins.
2. Add the red pepper flakes, tomatoes, broth, oregano, salt, and pepper. For 20 mins, simmer.
3. Use a standard blender or an immersion blender to combine soup up to it's smooth.
4. Add cream (if using) and basil and stir. Cook for an additional five mins.
5. Drizzle with more olive oil and serve warm.

Nutrition (Per Serving):

Cals: 180, Protein: 3g

Carbs: 20g

Fiber: 4g, Fat: 9g

8.CARROT AND GINGER SOUP

Prep Time: 15 mins
Cook Time: 25 mins
Total Time: 40 mins
Servings: 4

Ingredients:

- 1 tbsp olive oil
- 1 onion, chop-up
- 4 Big carrots, chop-up
- 1-inch piece fresh ginger, finely grated
- 3 cloves garlic, chop-up
- 4 cups of vegetable broth
- 1/2 tsp salt
- 1/4 tsp black pepper
- 1/2 tsp ground cumin
- 1/2 cup coconut milk (non-compulsory)
- Juice of 1/2 orange

Instructions:

1. In a Big saucepan, heat the olive oil over medium heat. Cook the carrots and onion for five mins.
2. Add cumin, salt, pepper, ginger, and garlic. For one min, stir.
3. Add the veggie broth. Carrots Must be tender after 20 mins of simmering.
4. Blend up to it's smooth. Add orange juice and coconut milk and stir.
5. Garnish with fresh herbs and serve warm.

Nutrition (Per Serving):

Cals: 160,Protein: 2g

Carbs: 20g

Fiber: 4g, Fat: 7g

Prep Time: 15 mins
Cook Time: 35 mins
Total Time: 50 mins
Servings: 6

Ingredients:

- 1 tbsp olive oil
- 1 onion, chop-up
- 2 carrots, diced
- 2 celery stalks, chop-up
- 3 cloves garlic, chop-up
- 1 zucchini, diced
- 1 can (14.5 oz) diced tomatoes
- 4 cups of vegetable broth
- 1 can (15 oz) kidney beans, drained
- 1 tsp dried oregano
- 1/2 tsp dried basil
- 1/2 tsp salt
- 1/4 tsp black pepper
- 1/2 cup whole wheat pasta
- 2 cups of spinach, chop-up

Instructions:

1. In a Big saucepan, heat the olive oil over medium heat. Add the garlic, celery, carrots, and onion. Cook for five mins.
2. Add the beans, tomatoes, oregano, basil, salt, pepper, and zucchini. For 20 mins, simmer.
3. Add pasta and simmer for 10 mins or up to it is tender.
4. Cook for two more mins after adding the spinach.
5. Garnish with Parmesan cheese or fresh basil and serve warm.

Nutrition (Per Serving):

Cals: 220, Protein: 9g

Carbs: 40g

Fiber: 8g, Fat: 4g

10.SPICY BLACK BEAN SOUP

Ingredients:

- 1 tbsp olive oil
- 1 onion, chop-up
- 1 red bell pepper, chop-up
- 3 cloves garlic, chop-up
- 1 tsp cumin
- 1/2 tsp smoked paprika
- 1/2 tsp chili powder
- 1/2 tsp salt
- 1/4 tsp cayenne pepper (non-compulsory)
- 2 cans (15 oz every) black beans, drained
- 3 cups of vegetable broth
- 1 can (14.5 oz) diced tomatoes
- Juice of 1 lime
- 1/4 cup fresh cilantro, chop-up

Instructions:

1. In a saucepan, heat the olive oil over medium heat. Cook for five mins after adding the bell pepper and onion.
2. Add the cayenne, chili powder, paprika, cumin, garlic, and salt. Cook for one min.
3. Add the tomatoes, broth, and black beans. For 20 mins, simmer.
4. To make the soup creamy, blend half of it.
5. Add cilantro and lime juice and stir. Warm up and serve.

Nutrition (Per Serving):

Cals: 250, Protein: 12g

Carbs: 40g

Fiber: 10g, Fat: 4g

11. KALE AND QUINOA SALAD WITH LEMON DRESSING

Prep Time: 15 mins
Cook Time: 15 mins

Total Time: 30 mins
Servings: 4

Ingredients:

- 1 cup quinoa, rinsed
- 2 cups of water
- 4 cups of kale, chop-up
- 1/2 cup cherry tomatoes, halved
- 1/4 cup red onion, thinly split
- 1/4 cup feta cheese, cut up
- 1/4 cup almonds, toasted
- 1/4 cup dried cranberries
- For the Lemon Dressing:
- 1/4 cup olive oil
- 2 tbsp lemon juice
- 1 tsp honey
- 1 tsp Dijon mustard
- Salt and pepper as needed

Instructions:

1. Bring water to a boil in a medium saucepan. Reduce the heat, add the quinoa, cover, and cook up to it's frothy, approximately 15 mins. Let to cool.
2. Massage the kale in a big bowl with a little olive oil for two mins to make it soft.
3. To the kale, add the cooked quinoa, feta cheese, red onion, cherry tomatoes, almonds, and cranberries.
4. Whisk the dressing ingredients in a mini bowl.
5. Pour over the salad and combine to combine.
6. Serve right away or store in the refrigerator for later.

Nutrition (Per Serving):

Cals: 280, Protein: 8g

Carbs: 35g

Fat: 12g, Fiber: 5g

12.MEDITERRANEAN CHICKPEA SALAD

Prep Time: 15 mins
Total Time: 15 mins
Servings: 4

Ingredients:

- 1 can (15 oz) chickpeas, drained and rinsed
- 1 cup cucumber, diced
- 1/2 cup cherry tomatoes, halved
- 1/4 cup red onion, lightly chop-up
- 1/4 cup Kalamata olives, split
- 1/4 cup feta cheese, cut up
- 1/4 cup parsley, chop-up
- For the Dressing:
- 3 tbsp olive oil
- 1 tbsp red wine vinegar
- 1 tsp lemon juice
- 1/2 tsp oregano
- Salt and pepper as needed

Instructions:

1. Chickpeas, cucumber, tomatoes, red onion, olives, feta, and parsley Must all be combined in a big dish.
2. Combine the olive oil, vinegar, lemon juice, oregano, salt, and pepper in a mini bowl.
3. Pour over the salad and combine thoroughly.
4. Serve right away or refrigerate before serving.

Nutrition (Per Serving):

Cals: 220, Protein: 7g

Carbs: 25g

Fat: 10g, Fiber: 6g

13.SPINACH SALAD WITH POMEGRANATE AND WALNUTS

Prep Time: 10 mins
Total Time: 10 mins
Servings: 4

Ingredients:

- 4 cups of baby spinach
- 1/2 cup pomegranate seeds
- 1/4 cup walnuts, toasted
- 1/4 cup feta cheese, cut up
- 1/4 cup red onion, thinly split
- For the Dressing:

- 3 tbsp olive oil
- 1 tbsp balsamic vinegar
- 1 tsp honey
- Salt and pepper as needed

Instructions:

1. Put the red onion, feta, walnuts, spinach, and pomegranate seeds in a big bowl.
2. Combine the olive oil, honey, balsamic vinegar, salt, and pepper in a mini bowl.
3. Pour over the salad and gently stir.
4. Serve right away.

Nutrition (Per Serving):

Cals: 180, Protein: 5g

Carbs: 15g

Fat: 12g, Fiber: 4g

14.GRILLED SALMON AND ARUGULA SALAD

Prep Time: 10 mins
Cook Time: 10 mins
Total Time: 20 mins
Servings: 2

Ingredients:

- 2 salmon fillets
- 4 cups of arugula
- 1/2 cup cherry tomatoes, halved
- 1/4 cup red onion, thinly split
- 1/4 cup avocado, split
- 1 tbsp olive oil (for grilling)
- For the Dressing:
- 3 tbsp olive oil
- 1 tbsp lemon juice
- 1 tsp Dijon mustard
- Salt and pepper as needed

Instructions:

1. Set the grill's temperature to medium-high.
2. Season salmon fillets with salt and pepper after brushing them with olive oil.

3. Salmon Must be cooked through after 3–4 mins on every side of the grill. Let to cool a little.
4. Put the avocado, red onion, cherry tomatoes, and arugula in a big bowl.
5. Combine the Dijon mustard, lemon juice, olive oil, salt, and pepper in a mini bowl.
6. Over the salad, flake the cooked salmon.
7. Gently combine the salad after adding the dressing.
8. Serve right away.

Nutrition (Per Serving):

Cals: 350, Protein: 30g

Carbs: 10g

Fat: 22g, Fiber: 3g

15.ROASTED BEET AND GOAT CHEESE SALAD

Prep Time: 10 mins
Cook Time: 40 mins
Total Time: 50 mins
Servings: 4

Ingredients:

- 3 medium beets, peel off and cubed
- 4 cups of combined greens
- 1/4 cup goat cheese, cut up
- 1/4 cup walnuts, toasted
- 1/4 cup balsamic glaze
- For the Dressing:
- 3 tbsp olive oil
- 1 tbsp balsamic vinegar
- 1 tsp honey
- Salt and pepper as needed

Instructions:

1. Turn the oven on to 400°F, or 200°C.
2. Put the beets on a baking sheet, pour some olive oil over them, and roast them for 35 to 40 mins, or up to they are soft. Let to cool.
3. Put the goat cheese, walnuts, roasted beets, and combined greens in a big bowl.
4. Combine the olive oil, honey, balsamic vinegar, salt, and pepper in a mini bowl.
5. Gently combine the salad after adding the dressing.
6. Before serving, drizzle balsamic glaze over the top.

Nutrition (Per Serving):

Cals: 200, Protein: 6g

Carbs: 20g

Fat: 12g, Fiber: 5g

16.OATMEAL WITH BERRIES AND FLAXSEEDS

Prep Time: 5 mins
Cook Time: 5 mins
Total Time: 10 mins
Servings: 1

Ingredients:

- ½ cup rolled oats
- 1 cup water or almond milk
- ½ cup combined berries (strawberries, blueberries, raspberries)
- 1 tbsp ground flaxseeds
- 1 tsp honey or maple syrup (non-compulsory)
- ½ tsp cinnamon (non-compulsory)

Instructions:

1. Bring water or almond milk to a boil in a saucepan.
2. Cook over medium heat, stirring periodically, for approximately five mins after adding the rolled oats.
3. Take off the heat and let it a min to settle.
4. If preferred, garnish with flaxseeds, honey or maple syrup, cinnamon, and combined berries.
5. Warm up and dig in!

Nutrition (Per Serving):

Cals: 250, Protein: 7g

Carbs: 45g

Fiber: 8g, Fat: 5g

17.AVOCADO TOAST WITH WHOLE GRAIN BREAD

Prep Time: 5 mins
Cook Time: 0 mins

Total Time: 5 mins
Servings: 1

Ingredients:

- 1 slice whole grain bread, toasted
- ½ ripe avocado
- ½ tsp lemon juice
- Salt and black pepper as needed
- ¼ tsp red pepper flakes (non-compulsory)
- 1 tsp olive oil (non-compulsory)
- Cherry tomatoes or microgreens for garnish

Instructions:

1. The whole grain bread Must be toasted till golden brown.
2. Mash the avocado, lemon juice, salt, and black pepper in a mini bowl.
3. Cover the toasted bread with the avocado Mixture.
4. If desired, top with red pepper flakes and drizzle with olive oil.
5. Add microgreens or cherry tomatoes as garnish.
6. Serve right away and savor!

Nutrition (Per Serving):

Cals: 220, Protein: 5g

Carbs: 24g

Fiber: 7g, Fat: 13g

18.SPINACH AND MUSHROOM EGG WHITE OMELET

Prep Time: 5 mins
Cook Time: 5 mins
Total Time: 10 mins
Servings: 1

Ingredients:

- 3 egg whites
- ½ cup fresh spinach, chop-up
- ¼ cup mushrooms, split
- 1 tbsp feta cheese (non-compulsory)
- ½ tsp olive oil
- Salt and black pepper as needed

Instructions:

1. In a nonstick skillet, heat the olive oil over medium heat.
2. Sauté the mushrooms for two mins up to they become tender.
3. Cook the spinach for one further min up to it wilts.
4. Add the egg whites and simmer for about two mins without stirring.
5. Cook for one more min after gently folding the omelet in half.
6. Serve right away and top with feta cheese, if using.

Nutrition (Per Serving):

Cals: 100, Protein: 14g

Carbs: 3g

Fiber: 1g, Fat: 3g

19.CHIA SEED PUDDING WITH ALMOND MILK

Prep Time: 5 mins
Cook Time: 0 mins (Chill Time: 2 hrs)
Total Time: 2 hrs 5 mins
Servings: 2

Ingredients:

- ¼ cup chia seeds
- 1 cup unsweetened almond milk
- 1 tsp honey or maple syrup
- ½ tsp vanilla extract
- ½ cup fresh berries (for topping)

Instructions:

1. Combine the chia seeds, almond milk, honey, and vanilla essence in a dish or jar.
2. After giving it a good stir, wait five mins. To avoid clumping, stir once more.
3. Refrigerate, covered, for at least two hrs or overnight.
4. Before serving, stir and sprinkle with fresh berries.
5. Savor it cold!

Nutrition (Per Serving):

Cals: 180, Protein: 5g

Carbs: 15g

Fiber: 8g, Fat: 9g

20.BANANA AND WALNUT WHOLE WHEAT PANCAKES

Prep Time: 10 mins
Cook Time: 10 mins
Total Time: 20 mins
Servings: 2

Ingredients:

- 1 ripe banana, mashed
- 1 cup whole wheat flour
- ½ cup milk (or almond milk)
- 1 tsp baking powder
- ½ tsp cinnamon
- 1 egg
- ¼ cup chop-up walnuts
- 1 tsp honey or maple syrup
- 1 tsp vanilla extract
- 1 tsp coconut oil (for cooking)

Instructions:

1. Mash the banana in a bowl and stir in the milk, honey, egg, and vanilla essence.
2. Add cinnamon, baking powder, and whole wheat flour. Stir just up to incorporated.
3. Add chop-up walnuts and fold.
4. Apply coconut oil to a nonstick skillet and cook it over medium heat.
5. After adding around ¼ cup of batter every pancake to the skillet, heat for two to three mins, or up to bubbles start to appear.
6. Cook for a further two mins after flipping, or up to golden brown.
7. If desired, top warm with more bananas and maple syrup.

Nutrition (Per Serving):

Cals: 320, Protein: 8g

Carbs: 45g

Fiber: 6g, Fat: 12g

21.GRILLED CHICKEN WITH AVOCADO SALSA

Prep Time: 10 mins
Cook Time: 15 mins

Total Time: 25 mins
Servings: 4

Ingredients

For the Chicken:

- 4 boneless, skinless chicken breasts
- 1 tbsp olive oil
- 1 tsp garlic powder
- 1 tsp onion powder
- 1 tsp paprika
- ½ tsp cumin
- ½ tsp salt
- ¼ tsp black pepper
- Juice of 1 lime

For the Avocado Salsa:

- 2 ripe avocados, diced
- 1 mini red onion, lightly chop-up
- 1 medium tomato, diced
- 1 tbsp cilantro, chop-up
- Juice of 1 lime
- Salt and pepper as needed

Instructions

1. Set the grill's temperature to medium-high.
2. Combine the lime juice, paprika, cumin, garlic powder, onion powder, olive oil, salt, and pepper in a mini bowl.
3. Coat the chicken breasts with the spice Mixture.
4. The chicken Must be cooked through (internal temperature of 165°F) after 6–7 mins on every side of the grill.
5. In a bowl, combine all the salsa ingredients while the chicken is roasting.
6. Serve the avocado salsa over the cooked chicken.

Nutrition (Per Serving)

Cals: 320, Protein: 38g

Carbs: 12g

Fat: 14g

22.TOFU AND BROCCOLI STIR-FRY

Ingredients

- 14 oz firm tofu, cubed
- 2 tbsp cornstarch
- 2 tbsp soy sauce
- 1 tbsp sesame oil
- 1 tbsp olive oil
- 3 cups of broccoli florets
- 1 red bell pepper, split
- 2 cloves garlic, chop-up
- 1 tsp ginger, chop-up
- 2 tbsp hoisin sauce
- 1 tbsp rice vinegar
- 1 tbsp sriracha (non-compulsory)
- 1 tsp sesame seeds (for garnish)

Instructions

1. Coat the tofu by tossing it with cornstarch.
2. Cook the tofu in a skillet with heated olive oil up to golden brown, about 5 mins on every side. Take out and put aside.
3. Add the bell pepper, ginger, garlic, broccoli, and sesame oil to the same pan. Stir-fry for three to four mins.
4. Stir in sriracha, rice vinegar, hoisin sauce, and soy sauce. Combine thoroughly.
5. Combine everything together and add the tofu back to the pan.
6. Garnish with sesame seeds and serve hot.

Nutrition (Per Serving)

Cals: 280, Protein: 15g

Carbs: 22g

Fat: 16g

23. CHICKPEA AND SPINACH CURRY

Prep Time: 10 mins
Cook Time: 20 mins
Total Time: 30 mins
Servings: 4

Ingredients

- 1 tbsp olive oil
- 1 onion, chop-up
- 2 cloves garlic, chop-up
- 1-inch piece ginger, finely grated
- 1 tsp cumin
- 1 tsp coriander
- 1 tsp turmeric
- 1 tsp garam masala
- 1 can (15 oz) chickpeas, drained
- 1 can (14 oz) diced tomatoes
- 1 cup coconut milk
- 2 cups of fresh spinach
- Salt and pepper as needed
- 1 tbsp lemon juice
- Cooked rice, for serving

Instructions

1. In a pan, heat the olive oil over medium heat. Saute the onion up to it becomes tender.
2. Add the garam masala, turmeric, coriander, cumin, ginger, and garlic. For one min, stir.
3. Add the coconut milk, tomatoes, and chickpeas. Simmer for ten mins.
4. Add the spinach and simmer for approximately two mins, or up to it has wilted.
5. Add lemon juice, salt, and pepper for seasoning. Serve over rice.

Nutrition (Per Serving)

Cals: 320, Protein: 10g

Carbs: 35g

Fat: 16g

24.BAKED FALAFEL WITH TAHINI SAUCE

Prep Time: 15 mins
Cook Time: 25 mins
Total Time: 40 mins
Servings: 4

Ingredients

For the Falafel:

- 1 can (15 oz) chickpeas, drained

- 1/2 onion, chop-up
- 2 cloves garlic, chop-up
- 2 tbsp fresh parsley, chop-up
- 1 tsp cumin
- 1 tsp coriander
- 1/2 tsp baking powder
- 3 tbsp flour
- Salt and pepper as needed
- 2 tbsp olive oil

For the Tahini Sauce:

- 1/4 cup tahini
- 2 tbsp lemon juice
- 1 clove garlic, chop-up
- 2-3 tbsp water
- Salt as needed

Instructions

1. Turn the oven on to 375°F, or 190°C.
2. In a mixer, blend all the falafel ingredients (omit olive oil) up to smooth.
3. Place on a baking sheet that has been prepared and form into little patties. Apply a little olive oil.
4. Bake for twenty to twenty-five mins, turning halfway through.
5. Blend all the components for the tahini sauce till it's smooth.
6. Serve tahini sauce alongside falafel.

Nutrition (Per Serving)

Cals: 290, Protein: 12g

Carbs: 35g

Fat: 12g

25. BLACK BEAN AND BROWN RICE BURRITOS

Prep Time: 10 mins
Cook Time: 15 mins
Total Time: 25 mins
Servings: 4

Ingredients

- 1 tbsp olive oil

- 1 onion, diced
- 1 clove garlic, chop-up
- 1 tsp cumin
- 1 tsp chili powder
- 1 can (15 oz) black beans, drained
- 1 cup cooked brown rice
- 1/2 cup corn kernels
- 1/2 cup diced tomatoes
- 4 Big whole wheat tortillas
- 1/2 cup shredded cheese (or vegan alternative)
- 1/4 cup chop-up cilantro
- Salsa, for serving

Instructions

1. In a pan, heat the olive oil. Sauté the garlic and onion up to they are tender.
2. Add rice, corn, tomatoes, black beans, cumin, and chili powder. Cook for five mins while stirring.
3. Divide the contents evenly among the warmed tortillas.
4. Before rolling into burritos, top with cheese and cilantro.
5. Serve with salsa.

Nutrition (Per Serving)

Cals: 350, Protein: 14g

Carbs: 50g

Fat: 10g

26.ROASTED BRUSSELS SPROUTS WITH BALSAMIC GLAZE

Prep Time: 10 mins
Cook Time: 25 mins
Total Time: 35 mins
Servings: 4

Ingredients:

- 1 lb Brussels sprouts, trimmed and halved
- 2 tbsp olive oil
- ½ tsp salt
- ¼ tsp black pepper
- 2 tbsp balsamic glaze

- 1 tbsp honey (non-compulsory)
- ¼ tsp red pepper flakes (non-compulsory)

Instructions:

1. Turn the oven on to 400°F, or 200°C.
2. Add salt, pepper, and olive oil to the Brussels sprouts.
3. Arrange them in a single layer on a baking sheet.
4. Roast up to golden brown, turning halfway through, 20 to 25 mins.
5. Before serving, drizzle with honey (if using) and balsamic glaze.

Nutrition (per serving):

Cals: 120, Carbs: 15g

Protein: 3g, Fat: 7g

Fiber: 4g

27.GARLIC MASHED CAULIFLOWER

Prep Time: 10 mins
Cook Time: 15 mins
Total Time: 25 mins
Servings: 4

Ingredients:

- 1 medium head cauliflower, slice into florets
- 2 tbsp butter or olive oil
- 3 cloves garlic, chop-up
- ¼ cup milk or broth
- ½ tsp salt
- ¼ tsp black pepper
- 2 tbsp finely grated Parmesan (non-compulsory)

Instructions:

1. Cauliflower Must be fork-tender after 10 to 15 mins of steaming or boiling.
2. Sauté garlic in butter in a skillet for one to two mins, or up to fragrant.
3. In a mixer, pulse the cauliflower, garlic, milk, salt, and pepper up to they are smooth.
4. Serve heated, stirring in Parmesan, if using.

Nutrition (per serving):

Cals: 90, Carbs: 9g

Protein: 3g, Fat: 6g

Fiber: 3g

28.QUINOA PILAF WITH NUTS AND DRIED FRUITS

Prep Time: 10 mins
Cook Time: 20 mins
Total Time: 30 mins
Servings: 4

Ingredients:

- 1 cup quinoa, rinsed
- 2 cups of vegetable broth
- ½ cup combined nuts (almonds, walnuts, pecans), chop-up
- ½ cup dried fruits (raisins, cranberries, apricots), chop-up
- 1 tbsp olive oil
- ½ mini onion, lightly chop-up
- 1 tsp cumin
- ½ tsp cinnamon
- ¼ tsp salt

Instructions:

1. In a saucepan, heat the olive oil over medium heat and cook the onions for two to three mins.
2. Stir for one min after adding the quinoa, salt, cinnamon, and cumin.
3. Add the vegetable stock, bring to a boil, lower the heat, and simmer the quinoa for 15 mins to cook it.
4. Using a fork, fluff in the nuts and dried fruits, then serve warm.

Nutrition (per serving):

Cals: 250, Carbs: 40g

Protein: 7g, Fat: 9g

Fiber: 5g

29.SAUTÉED SPINACH WITH GARLIC

Prep Time: 5 mins
Cook Time: 5 mins
Total Time: 10 mins
Servings: 4

Ingredients:

- 1 lb fresh spinach
- 1 tbsp olive oil
- 3 cloves garlic, chop-up
- ½ tsp salt
- ¼ tsp black pepper
- ¼ tsp red pepper flakes (non-compulsory)

Instructions:

1. In a Big pan, heat the olive oil over medium heat.
2. Sauté the garlic for 30 seconds till it becomes aromatic.
3. Cook the spinach for two to three mins, stirring regularly, up to it wilts.
4. Add salt, black pepper, and, if needed, red pepper flakes for seasoning.
5. Serve right away.

Nutrition (per serving):

Cals: 70, Carbs: 5g

Protein: 3g, Fat: 5g

Fiber: 2g

30.SWEET POTATO WEDGES WITH PAPRIKA

Prep Time: 10 mins
Cook Time: 30 mins
Total Time: 40 mins
Servings: 4

Ingredients:

- 2 Big sweet potatoes, slice into wedges
- 2 tbsp olive oil
- 1 tsp paprika
- ½ tsp salt
- ¼ tsp black pepper
- ¼ tsp garlic powder (non-compulsory)

Instructions:

1. Set the oven temperature to 425°F (220°C).
2. Add salt, pepper, paprika, and olive oil to sweet potato wedges.
3. Line a baking sheet with an equal layer.
4. Roast up to golden brown and crispy, turning halfway through, 25 to 30 mins.

5. Warm up and serve.

Nutrition (per serving):

Cals: 160, Carbs: 30g

Protein: 2g, Fat: 5g

Fiber: 4g

31.HUMMUS WITH CARROT AND CUCUMBER STICKS

Prep Time: 10 mins
Cook Time: 0 mins
Total Time: 10 mins
Servings: 4

Ingredients:

For the Hummus:

- 1 can (15 oz) chickpeas, drained and rinsed
- 3 tbsp tahini
- 2 tbsp lemon juice
- 1 clove garlic, chop-up
- 2 tbsp olive oil
- ½ tsp ground cumin
- ¼ tsp salt
- 2–3 tbsp water (as needed for consistency)

For Serving:

- 2 Big carrots, slice into sticks
- 1 cucumber, slice into sticks

Instructions:

1. Put the chickpeas, tahini, lemon juice, cumin, olive oil, garlic, and salt in a mixer.
2. Add water a little at a time up to the desired consistency is achieved, then blend up to smooth.
3. If desired, sprinkle with a little more olive oil after transferring to a bowl.
4. Serve with cucumber and carrot sticks.

Nutrition (Per Serving):

Cals: 190, Protein: 6g

Carbs: 18g

Fiber: 5g, Fat: 10g

32.AIR-POPPED POPCORN WITH NUTRITIONAL YEAST

Prep Time: 5 mins
Cook Time: 5 mins
Total Time: 10 mins
Servings: 4

Ingredients:

- ½ cup popcorn kernels
- 2 tbsp nutritional yeast
- 1 tbsp olive oil (non-compulsory)
- ¼ tsp salt

Instructions:

1. Use an air popper to pop the popcorn.
2. Popcorn Must be moved to a big bowl.
3. If using, drizzle with olive oil, then top with salt and nutritional yeast.
4. Serve right away after tossing thoroughly.

Nutrition (Per Serving):

Cals: 100, Protein: 4g

Carbs: 18g

Fiber: 4g, Fat: 2g

33.ROASTED CHICKPEAS WITH SPICES

Prep Time: 5 mins
Cook Time: 30 mins
Total Time: 35 mins
Servings: 4

Ingredients:

- 1 can (15 oz) chickpeas, drained and rinsed
- 1 tbsp olive oil
- ½ tsp salt

- ½ tsp smoked paprika
- ½ tsp cumin
- ¼ tsp black pepper

Instructions:

1. Turn the oven on to 400°F, or 200°C.
2. Use paper towels to pat the chickpeas dry.
3. Add salt, paprika, cumin, black pepper, and olive oil and toss.
4. Arrange on a baking sheet in a single layer.
5. Roast up to crispy, stirring the pan halfway through, 25 to 30 mins.
6. Before serving, let it cool somewhat.

Nutrition (Per Serving):

Cals: 150, Protein: 6g

Carbs: 20g

Fiber: 5g, Fat: 5g

34.ALMOND AND BERRY TRAIL COMBINE

Prep Time: 5 mins
Cook Time: 0 mins
Total Time: 5 mins
Servings: 4

Ingredients:

- ½ cup almonds
- ½ cup cashews
- ½ cup dried cranberries
- ½ cup dried blueberries
- ¼ cup sunflower seeds

Instructions:

1. Combine all ingredients in a bowl.
2. Up to it's time to serve, keep it in an airtight container.

Nutrition (Per Serving):

Cals: 200, Protein: 6g

Carbs: 18g

Fiber: 4g, Fat: 12g

35. GREEK YOGURT WITH HONEY AND NUTS

Prep Time: 5 mins
Cook Time: 0 mins
Total Time: 5 mins
Servings: 4

Ingredients:

- 2 cups of Greek yogurt
- 2 tbsp honey
- ¼ cup chop-up walnuts
- ¼ cup chop-up almonds

Instructions:

1. Greek yogurt Must be slice up among four bowls.
2. Evenly drizzle every dish with honey.
3. Add chop-up almonds and walnuts on top.
4. Serve right away.

Nutrition (Per Serving):

Cals: 180, Protein: 12g

Carbs: 14g

Fiber: 2g, Fat: 8g

36. GREEN SMOOTHIE WITH SPINACH AND AVOCADO

Prep Time: 5 mins
Cook Time: 0 mins
Total Time: 5 mins
Servings: 2

Ingredients:

- 1 cup fresh spinach
- ½ avocado, peel off and pitted
- 1 banana
- 1 cup almond milk (or any milk of choice)
- ½ cup Greek yogurt (non-compulsory for creaminess)
- 1 tbsp chia seeds

- 1 tsp honey or maple syrup (non-compulsory)
- ½ cup ice cubes

Instructions:

1. Put everything in a blender.
2. Blend till creamy and smooth.
3. If necessary, taste and adjust the sweetness.
4. Serve right away after pouring into glasses.

Nutrition (Per Serving):

Cals: 180, Protein: 5g

Carbs: 25g

Fiber: 6g, Fat: 7g

37.BLUEBERRY ALMOND BUTTER SMOOTHIE

Prep Time: 5 mins
Cook Time: 0 mins
Total Time: 5 mins
Servings: 2

Ingredients:

- 1 cup refrigerate blueberries
- 1 banana
- 1 cup unsweetened almond milk
- 2 tbsp almond butter
- 1 tsp vanilla extract
- 1 tsp honey (non-compulsory)
- ½ cup ice cubes

Instructions:

1. Put everything in a blender.
2. Blend till creamy and smooth.
3. Serve right away after pouring into glasses.

Nutrition (Per Serving):

Cals: 220, Protein: 6g

Carbs: 28g

Fiber: 5g, Fat: 10g

38.GOLDEN TURMERIC LATTE

Prep Time: 5 mins
Cook Time: 5 mins
Total Time: 10 mins
Servings: 2

Ingredients:

- 2 cups of unsweetened almond milk (or any milk of choice)
- 1 tsp turmeric powder
- ½ tsp ground cinnamon
- ¼ tsp ground ginger
- 1 tsp honey or maple syrup
- ½ tsp vanilla extract
- A pinch of black pepper (enhances turmeric absorption)

Instructions:

1. Whisk all ingredients together in a mini saucepan over medium heat.
2. Do not boil; just heat up to warm.
3. Transfer to cups of and serve hot.

Nutrition (Per Serving):

Cals: 90, Protein: 2g

Carbs: 12g

Fiber: 1g, Fat: 4g

39.HIBISCUS TEA WITH LEMON

Prep Time: 5 mins
Cook Time: 10 mins
Total Time: 15 mins
Servings: 4

Ingredients:

- 4 cups of water
- ¼ cup dried hibiscus flowers
- 1 tbsp honey or sugar (non-compulsory)
- Juice of 1 lemon
- Ice cubes (for serving, non-compulsory)

Instructions:

1. In a saucepan, bring water to a boil.
2. After taking off the heat, add the dried hibiscus blossoms.
3. After 10 mins of steeping, strain.
4. If using, stir in the sweetener and lemon juice.
5. Serve warm over ice or cold.

Nutrition (Per Serving):

Cals: 25, Protein: 0g

Carbs: 6g

Fiber: 0g, Fat: 0g

40.WATERMELON AND MINT INFUSED WATER

Prep Time: 10 mins
Total Time: 10 mins
Servings: 4

Ingredients

- 4 cups of watermelon, cubed
- 10-12 fresh mint leaves
- 4 cups of cold water
- 1 cup ice cubes

Instructions

1. Fill a big pitcher with watermelon cubes and mint leaves.
2. Cover the ingredients with cold water.
3. To infuse flavors, let it rest for at least half an hr.
4. To serve, add ice cubes.

Nutrition (Per Serving)

Cals: 15, Carbs: 4g

Protein: 0g, Fat: 0g

Fiber: 0g, Sugar: 3g

41.DARK CHOCOLATE AVOCADO MOUSSE

Ingredients

- 1 ripe avocado
- 3 tbsp unsweetened cocoa powder
- 2 tbsp maple syrup or honey
- 1 tsp vanilla extract
- ¼ cup almond milk (adjust for consistency)
- A pinch of sea salt

Instructions

1. In a mixer, blend all the ingredients up to they are smooth.
2. If necessary, adjust the thickness or sweetness.
3. Before serving, let it cool for ten mins.

Nutrition (Per Serving)

Cals: 180, Carbs: 20g

Protein: 3g, Fat: 12g

Fiber: 6g, Sugar: 10g

42.CHIA SEED PUDDING WITH MANGO

Prep Time: 5 mins
Chill Time: 4 hrs
Total Time: 4 hrs 5 mins
Servings: 2

Ingredients

- ¼ cup chia seeds
- 1 cup almond milk
- 1 tbsp maple syrup or honey
- ½ tsp vanilla extract
- ½ cup diced mango

Instructions

1. In a dish, combine chia seeds, almond milk, vanilla, and sweetener.
2. Give everything a good stir, then put it in the fridge for at least four hrs or overnight.
3. Before serving, sprinkle some chop-up mango on top.

Nutrition (Per Serving)

Cals: 180, Carbs: 20g

Protein: 5g, Fat: 8g

Fiber: 7g, Sugar: 10g

43.BAKED APPLES WITH CINNAMON AND WALNUTS

Prep Time: 10 mins
Cook Time: 25 mins
Total Time: 35 mins
Servings: 4

Ingredients

- 4 apples, cored
- ¼ cup chop-up walnuts
- 2 tbsp maple syrup or honey
- 1 tsp cinnamon
- ½ tsp vanilla extract

Instructions

1. Turn the oven on to 375°F, or 190°C.
2. In a bowl, combine walnuts, maple syrup, cinnamon, and vanilla.
3. Stuff the Mixture into apples.
4. Apples Must be soft after 25 mins in the oven.

Nutrition (Per Serving)

Cals: 150, Carbs: 32g

Protein: 2g, Fat: 4g

Fiber: 5g, Sugar: 25g

44.OATMEAL RAISIN COOKIES WITH ALMOND BUTTER

Prep Time: 10 mins
Cook Time: 12 mins
Total Time: 22 mins
Servings: 12 cookies

Ingredients

- 1 cup rolled oats
- ½ cup almond butter
- ¼ cup maple syrup or honey
- ¼ cup raisins
- ½ tsp cinnamon
- ½ tsp vanilla extract

Instructions

1. Set the oven temperature to 175°C (350°F).
2. In a bowl, thoroughly combine all the ingredients.
3. Place the dough onto a baking sheet and gently press it down.
4. Bake up to golden brown, 12 mins.

Nutrition (Per Cookie)

Cals: 100, Carbs: 12g

Protein: 2g, Fat: 5g

Fiber: 2g, Sugar: 6g

45.GREEK YOGURT WITH COMBINED BERRIES AND HONEY

Prep Time: 5 mins
Total Time: 5 mins
Servings: 2

Ingredients

- 1 cup Greek yogurt
- ½ cup combined berries (strawberries, blueberries, raspberries)
- 1 tbsp honey
- 1 tbsp chop-up nuts (non-compulsory)

Instructions

1. Greek yogurt Must be slice up between two bowls.
2. Drizzle honey over top, garnish with combined berries, and, if using, add nuts.

Nutrition (Per Serving)

Cals: 150, Carbs: 20g

Protein: 12g, Fat: 3g

Fiber: 3g, Sugar: 15g

46.BANANA ICE CREAM WITH CACAO NIBS

Prep Time: 5 mins
Cook Time: 0 mins
Total Time: 5 mins (+ freezing time)
Servings: 2

Ingredients:

- 2 ripe bananas, split and refrigerate
- 1/2 tsp vanilla extract
- 2 tbsp cacao nibs
- 2 tbsp almond milk (if needed for blending)

Instructions:

1. Put the refrigerate banana slices in a mixer or blender.
2. Blend, scraping down sides as necessary, up to smooth. Add almond milk a little at a time if the Mixture is too thick.
3. Add cacao nibs and stir.
4. For a soft-serve texture, serve right away; for a stiffer consistency, freeze for one hr.

Nutrition (Per Serving):

Cals: 150, Protein: 2g

Carbs: 35g

Fat: 2g, Fiber: 4g

Sugar: 18g

47.PUMPKIN MUFFINS WITH WHOLE WHEAT FLOUR

Prep Time: 10 mins
Cook Time: 20 mins
Total Time: 30 mins
Servings: 12 muffins

Ingredients:

- 1 1/2 cups of whole wheat flour

- 1 tsp baking soda
- 1/2 tsp salt
- 1 tsp cinnamon
- 1/2 tsp nutmeg
- 1/4 tsp ginger
- 1 cup canned pumpkin puree
- 1/2 cup honey or maple syrup
- 2 eggs
- 1/4 cup coconut oil, dilute
- 1/4 cup almond milk
- 1 tsp vanilla extract

Instructions:

1. Set the oven temperature to 175°C (350°F). Put liners inside a muffin tray.
2. Combine the flour, baking soda, salt, ginger, cinnamon, and nutmeg in a bowl.
3. Combine the pureed pumpkin, honey, eggs, almond milk, coconut oil, and vanilla in a separate dish.
4. Combine the dry ingredients into the wet ones gradually.
5. After dividing the batter into muffin cups of, bake them for 18 to 20 mins.
6. Before serving, let it cool.

Nutrition (Per Muffin):

Cals: 150, Protein: 3g

Carbs: 25g

Fat: 5g, Fiber: 3g

Sugar: 10g

48.ALMOND AND DATE ENERGY BALLS

Prep Time: 10 mins
Cook Time: 0 mins
Total Time: 10 mins
Servings: 12 energy balls

Ingredients:

- 1 cup almonds
- 1 cup pitted dates
- 2 tbsp cocoa powder
- 1 tsp vanilla extract
- 1/2 tsp cinnamon

- 1 tbsp water (if needed)

Instructions:

1. Pulse the almonds in a mixer up to they are lightly crushed.
2. Add cinnamon, vanilla, cocoa powder, and dates. Blend the ingredients up to it comes together.
3. One tbsp of water can be added if necessary to help the Mixture bond.
4. Before serving, roll into little balls and chill for at least half an hr.

Nutrition (Per Ball):

Cals: 90, Protein: 2g

Carbs: 12g

Fat: 4g, Fiber: 2g

Sugar: 8g

49.COCONUT CHIA PUDDING

Prep Time: 5 mins
Cook Time: 0 mins
Total Time: 4 hrs (chilling time)
Servings: 2

Ingredients:

- 1 cup coconut milk
- 1/4 cup chia seeds
- 1 tbsp maple syrup or honey
- 1/2 tsp vanilla extract
- Fresh fruit for topping (non-compulsory)

Instructions:

1. Combine the chia seeds, coconut milk, vanilla, and sweetener in a bowl.
2. After giving it a good stir, wait five mins. To avoid clumping, stir once more.
3. For at least four hrs or overnight, cover and place in the refrigerator.
4. Before serving, stir and, if wanted, garnish with fresh fruit.

Nutrition (Per Serving):

Cals: 200, Protein: 3g

Carbs: 12g

Fat: 14g, Fiber: 5g

Sugar: 5g

50.DARK CHOCOLATE-COVERED STRAWBERRIES

Prep Time: 10 mins
Cook Time: 5 mins
Total Time: 15 mins
Servings: 12 strawberries

Ingredients:

- 12 fresh strawberries, washed and dried
- 3 ozs dark chocolate (70% cocoa or higher), chop-up
- 1 tsp coconut oil (non-compulsory)

Instructions:

1. In a microwave-safe dish, melt the dark chocolate and coconut oil (if using) in 20-second increments while stirring.
2. Let extra chocolate to drop off after dipping every strawberry into the dilute chocolate.
3. Transfer to a pan lined with parchment paper and chill for approximately ten mins or up to the chocolate solidifies.
4. Serve right away or keep refrigerated.

Nutrition (Per Strawberry):

Cals: 50, Protein: 1g

Carbs: 7g

Fat: 3g, Fiber: 1g

Sugar: 5g

51.MEDITERRANEAN QUINOA SALAD

Prep Time: 15 mins
Cook Time: 15 mins
Total Time: 30 mins
Servings: 4

Ingredients:

- 1 cup quinoa, rinsed
- 2 cups of water

- 1 cup cherry tomatoes, halved
- 1/2 cucumber, diced
- 1/4 red onion, lightly chop-up
- 1/4 cup Kalamata olives, split
- 1/4 cup feta cheese, cut up
- 2 tbsp olive oil
- 1 tbsp lemon juice
- 1 tsp dried oregano
- Salt and pepper as needed

Instructions:

1. Heat water in a medium pot up to it boils. Reduce the heat, cover, and cook the quinoa for 15 mins, or up to the water has been absorbed. Using a fork, fluff and let to cool.
2. Quinoa, tomatoes, cucumber, red onion, olives, and feta cheese Must all be combined in a big dish.
3. Combine the olive oil, lemon juice, oregano, salt, and pepper in a mini bowl.
4. Drizzle the salad with the dressing and toss to combine.
5. You may serve it cold or warm.

Nutrition (Per Serving):

Cals: 250, Protein: 8g

Carbs: 35g, Fat: 10g

Fiber: 5g

52.GRILLED SALMON WITH LEMON-DILL SAUCE

Prep Time: 10 mins
Cook Time: 15 mins
Total Time: 25 mins
Servings: 4

Ingredients:

- 4 salmon fillets (6 oz every)
- 1 tbsp olive oil
- 1 tsp salt
- 1/2 tsp black pepper
- 1 tbsp lemon juice
- 1 tsp garlic powder
- 1 tsp paprika

For the Lemon-Dill Sauce:

- 1/2 cup Greek yogurt
- 1 tbsp fresh dill, chop-up
- 1 tbsp lemon juice
- 1 tsp honey
- Salt and pepper as needed

Instructions:

1. Set the grill's temperature to medium-high.
2. Season salmon fillets with salt, pepper, lemon juice, garlic powder, and paprika after brushing them with olive oil.
3. Salmon Must be opaque and flaky after grilling for 4–5 mins on every side.
4. Combine the Greek yogurt, dill, lemon juice, honey, salt, and pepper in a mini bowl.
5. Top with the lemon-dill sauce and serve the salmon.

Nutrition (Per Serving):

Cals: 320, Protein: 35g

Carbs: 5g, Fat: 18g

Fiber: 0g

53.AVOCADO AND BLACK BEAN WRAP

Prep Time: 10 mins
Cook Time: 0 mins
Total Time: 10 mins
Servings: 2

Ingredients:

- 2 whole wheat tortillas
- 1 avocado, mashed
- 1/2 cup black beans, drained and rinsed
- 1/4 cup cherry tomatoes, diced
- 1/4 cup shredded lettuce
- 2 tbsp Greek yogurt
- 1 tbsp lime juice
- 1/2 tsp cumin
- Salt and pepper as needed

Instructions:

1. Mash the avocado and combine it with the lime juice, cumin, salt, and pepper in a mini bowl.

2. On every tortilla, spread the mashed avocado.
3. Add Greek yogurt, shredded lettuce, cherry tomatoes, and black beans over top.
4. After securely rolling the tortillas, slice them in half.
5. Serve right away.

Nutrition (Per Serving):

Cals: 280, Protein: 8g

Carbs: 38g, Fat: 12g

Fiber: 9g

54.OATMEAL WITH BERRIES AND NUTS

Prep Time: 5 mins
Cook Time: 5 mins
Total Time: 10 mins
Servings: 2

Ingredients:

- 1 cup rolled oats
- 2 cups of almond milk (or water)
- 1 tbsp honey or maple syrup
- 1/2 tsp cinnamon
- 1/2 cup combined berries (strawberries, blueberries, raspberries)
- 2 tbsp chop-up nuts (almonds, walnuts, or pecans)
- 1/2 tsp vanilla extract

Instructions:

1. Heat the almond milk in a saucepan up to it boils. Turn the heat down to low and add the oats.
2. Cook up to thick and creamy, stirring regularly, for 5 mins.
3. Add vanilla essence, honey, and cinnamon and stir.
4. Before serving, sprinkle chop-up nuts and berries over top.

Nutrition (Per Serving):

Cals: 270, Protein: 7g, Carbs: 45g

Fat: 8g, Fiber: 6g

55.SPINACH AND CHICKPEA STIR-FRY

Prep Time: 5 mins
Cook Time: 10 mins
Total Time: 15 mins
Servings: 4

Ingredients:

- 1 tbsp olive oil
- 1/2 onion, split
- 2 cloves garlic, chop-up
- 1 can (15 oz) chickpeas, drained and rinsed
- 4 cups of fresh spinach
- 1 tsp cumin
- 1/2 tsp paprika
- Salt and pepper as needed
- 1 tbsp lemon juice

Instructions:

1. In a pan, heat the olive oil over medium heat. Cook the onion up to it becomes tender.
2. Cook for 30 seconds after adding the garlic.
3. Add the paprika, cumin, chickpeas, salt, and pepper and stir. Cook, stirring periodically, for 5 mins.
4. Cook the spinach for about two mins, or up to it has wilted.
5. Before serving, take off the heat and squeeze in some lemon juice.

Nutrition (Per Serving):

Cals: 180, Protein: 7g

Carbs: 24g, Fat: 6g

Fiber: 6g

56.EASY CHICKEN PARMESAN

Prep Time: 15 mins
Cook Time: 25 mins
Total Time: 40 mins
Servings: 4

Ingredients:

- 4 boneless, skinless chicken breasts
- ½ cup flour
- 2 Big eggs, beaten

- 1 cup panko breadcrumbs
- ½ cup finely grated Parmesan cheese
- 1 cup marinara sauce
- 1 ½ cups of shredded mozzarella cheese
- 2 tbsp olive oil
- Salt and pepper as needed

Instructions:

1. Turn the oven on to 375°F, or 190°C.
2. To get a uniform thickness, lb the chicken breasts. Add salt and pepper for seasoning.
3. Coat every breast with a combination of breadcrumbs and Parmesan cheese after dredging it in flour and dipping it into beaten eggs.
4. In a pan, heat the olive oil over medium heat. Cook up to golden on all sides, 2 to 3 mins per side.
5. The chicken Must be put in a baking dish. Add mozzarella cheese and marinara sauce on top.
6. Bake for 20 mins, or up to the cheese has dilute and the chicken is cooked through.

Nutrition (per serving):

Cals: 420, Protein: 40g

Carbs: 15g

Fat: 20g, Fiber: 2g

57.VYPRÁŽANÉ KURACIE PRSIA (FRIED CHICKEN BREASTS)

Prep Time: 15 mins

Cook Time: 15 mins

Total Time: 30 mins

Servings: 4

Ingredients:

- 4 boneless, skinless chicken breasts
- 1 cup all-purpose flour
- 2 eggs, beaten
- 1 cup breadcrumbs
- Salt and pepper as needed
- Vegetable oil, for frying

Instructions:

1. Sandwich the chicken breasts between two plastic wrap sheets. Roll them out or lb them with a meat mallet to a uniform thickness.
2. Add salt and pepper to the chicken breasts for seasoning.
3. Three shlet dishes Must be set up: one for flour, one for beaten eggs, and one for breadcrumbs.
4. Every chicken breast Must first be coated in flour, then dipped in whisked eggs, and finally covered in breadcrumbs, gently pressed to cling.
5. In a big skillet, heat the vegetable oil over medium-high heat.
6. The chicken breasts Must be cooked through and golden brown after 5 to 6 mins of frying on every side.
7. Take out of the skillet and put on a dish covered with paper towels to absorb extra oil.
8. Warm up and pair with your preferred sides. Have fun!

Nutrition (per serving):

Cals: 380, Protein: 30g

Fat: 12g, Carbs: 35g

Fiber: 2g

58. CESNAKOVÉ KURACIE STEAKY (GARLIC CHICKEN STEAKS)

Prep Time: 10 mins

Cook Time: 20 mins

Total Time: 30 mins

Servings: 4

Ingredients:

- 4 boneless, skinless chicken breasts
- 4 cloves garlic, chop-up
- 2 tbsp olive oil
- 1/2 tsp paprika
- Salt and pepper as needed
- Fresh parsley, chop-up, for garnish

Instructions:

1. Turn the oven on to 375°F, or 190°C.
2. Add paprika, salt, and pepper to the chicken breasts' seasoning.
3. Heat the olive oil in a skillet that is ovensafe to medium-high heat.

4. Garlic powder Must be added to the skillet and cooked for about one min, or up to aromatic.
5. The seasoned chicken breasts Must be seared for two to three mins on every side, or up to they are golden brown.
6. Place the skillet in the oven that has been preheated, and bake for 12 to 15 mins, or up to the chicken is thoroughly done.
7. Before serving, garnish with chop-up parsley. Have fun!

Nutrition (per serving):

Cals: 290, Protein: 30g

Fat: 14g, Carbs: 4g

Fiber: 1g

59.HOVÄDZIA STEAKY S HLIVOU (BEEF STEAKS WITH MUSHROOMS)

Prep Time: 15 mins

Cook Time: 20 mins

Total Time: 35 mins

Servings: 4

Ingredients:

- 4 beef steaks (about 6 oz every)
- 2 cups of split mushrooms
- 2 cloves garlic, chop-up
- 2 tbsp olive oil
- Salt and pepper as needed

Instructions:

1. On both sides, season the beef steaks with salt and pepper.
2. In a big skillet set over medium-high heat, warm the olive oil.
3. To get medium-rare, add the beef steaks to the skillet and cook for about 4–5 mins on every side, or up to done to your taste. After taking the steaks out of the skillet, set them aside.
4. Add the chop-up garlic and the split mushrooms to the same skillet. Simmer the mushrooms for 5 to 7 mins, or up to they are soft.
5. Enjoy the meat steaks with the sautéed mushrooms on top!

NUTRITION INFO: (per serving)

Cals: 350, Protein: 30g

Fat: 22g, Carbs: 5g

Fiber: 2g

60. VYPRÁŽANÉ BRAVČOVÉ KÚSKY (FRIED PORK PIECES)

Prep Time: 10 mins

Cook Time: 20 mins

Total Time: 30 mins

Servings: 4

Ingredients:

- 1 lb pork loin, slice into bite-sized pieces
- 1 cup all-purpose flour
- 2 eggs, beaten
- 1 cup breadcrumbs
- Salt and pepper as needed
- Vegetable oil for frying

Instructions:

1. Add salt and pepper to the pork chunks for seasoning.
2. Three shlet dishes Must be set up: one for flour, one for beaten eggs, and one for breadcrumbs.
3. Every piece of pork Must be first coated with flour, then dipped in beaten eggs, and then covered with breadcrumbs.
4. In a big skillet, heat the vegetable oil over medium-high heat.
5. Fry the breaded pork pieces in batches for 4–5 mins on every side, or up to they are cooked through and golden brown.
6. After taking the crispy pork chunks out of the skillet, pat dry using paper towels.
7. Serve hot with your preferred side dishes or dipping sauce.

NUTRITION INFO: (per serving)

Cals: 380, Protein: 25g

Fat: 15g, Carbs: 30g, Fiber: 2g

Made in United States
North Haven, CT
28 May 2025

69286817R00030